WHAT IS TOMMY
THINKING?

Stories Based on the Gospel
Readings for Sunday, Cycle A

PASTOR GIL SPLETT

WESTBOW
PRESS®
A DIVISION OF THOMAS NELSON
& ZONDERVAN

WestBow Press books may be ordered through booksellers or by contacting:

WestBow Press
A Division of Thomas Nelson & Zondervan
1663 Liberty Drive
Bloomington, IN 47403
www.westbowpress.com
1 (866) 928-1240

ISBN: 978-1-5127-6524-3 (sc)
ISBN: 978-1-5127-6523-6 (hc)
ISBN: 978-1-5127-6525-0 (e)

Library of Congress Control Number: 2016919395

Print information available on the last page.

WestBow Press rev. date: 12/01/2016

Dedicated to my Children

Kathryn, Paul, Gilbert Timothy

Who became some of my best friends

Introduction

Early in my ministry, I discovered that my sermons for children were often more humorous than informative. Preschool children were difficult to predict, and it was a challenge to hold their attention and at the same time engage the older children.

As a solution, I turned to a hobby of mine: drawing pictures. I decided to use a character I had created when I was in seminary called Tommy, named after the disciple Thomas. Thomas is often called "Doubting Thomas," but I find him to be not so much a doubter as a good questioner. Tommy asks a lot of questions, as many ten-year-olds do. It is my intention to have him ask questions that are on the minds of many grade school children.

This book of sixty-three stories and sixty-three pictures is based on the Revised Common Lectionary, a three-year cycle of scripture readings developed by the Consultation on Common Texts with twenty member churches. This book consists of the Gospel readings for Cycle A, the first year in the three-year cycle.

My focus age is eight, and I prepare the stories thinking of third graders, perhaps because that was one of my own favorite years in school. It was during World War II, and I was elected to sell the savings bond stamps—my first big responsibility. I have tried to make Tommy's context more contemporary, although I do sometimes fall back to the childhood with which I am more familiar. Usually, that's my own children's context, which was the late sixties and early seventies.

While the focus of the stories may not address the main point of the text you would hear shared in the adult sermon, I have always tried to focus on questions and issues that may be in the mind of a child and to provide insight and theology that will stand up when the child goes off to college.

Please share these stories with your children and, if possible, continue the conversation with them. It is a great opportunity for you to share your faith. I remember a month or so after my first child started Sunday school, she was singing that favorite children's hymn, "Jesus Loves Me." Only instead of ending with, "For the Bible tells me so," she sang, "For my daddy tells me so." I feel certain that will be true for your children also.

You will notice that the Eighth Sunday after Epiphany is the same lesson as Lectionary Eight. That is because the season of Epiphany can be as short as four Sundays and as many as eight, depending on when Easter falls, which can be as early as late March or as late as late April. The Sundays after Pentecost are designated as Lectionary 8–33: the number 8 for Sunday May 24 through May 28, and number 9 for Sunday May 29 through June 4, etc. However, if Easter is very late, the first Sunday after Holy Trinity would be Lectionary 13

I hope you will find as much pleasure in reading these stories as I have enjoyed in creating them.

Gilbert Splett
June 11, 2016

Foreword

Someone once asked me what the hardest part of my vocation is. The answer came in a flash: preaching to children. Children must be children, after all. They can be inattentive, squirmy, and way too literal. And how does one speak of the Paschal mystery, the death and resurrection of Jesus, and the gracious love of God in a way that children can understand?

Yet so much of our ministry is spent with children. And they are the future of our church. We are challenged to pay attention to this important ministry. Week after week, young families come to the faith community for sustenance, for a word that will inspire them and challenge them. Don't these young hearts deserve to be inspired and challenged as well?

Pastor Gil Splett, in his stories of Tommy, does just that: he pays attention to the proclamation of the gospel; he pays attention to the love of God that comes to us in Jesus; he pays attention to children.

With insightfulness, artistry, and grace, Pastor Gil Splett weaves stories that children can understand, stories that allow adults to listen in and enter more deeply into the Paschal mystery. Whether he writes (and draws!) of Tommy stumbling in the dark at scout camp and learning about the light of Christ that guides him, or lying on the grass looking up at the stars and reflecting on the largeness of heaven, Tommy always has something to learn—and more, something to pass on to other children. I have personally witnessed Pastor Gil weaving his craft. Children identify with Tommy, the little boy with a big heart who plays like them, questions and learns like them, and is always surprised like them. Children enjoy listening as Pastor Gil shares his Tommy stories and watches in awe as he draws the story for them on a whiteboard, allowing Tommy to come alive right before their eyes. What a wonderful way to preach to children—to preach to all of us.

I invite you to read these stories of Tommy and allow your heart to once again be opened to the good news. Perhaps if you are a pastor or a religious educator, you will choose to use them in your work with children. Perhaps in reading, you will recover your inner child, the child claimed by God at your baptism. These stories will make you smile. These stories will challenge you. These stories will offer you good news.

Pastor Jeff Vanden Heuvel
Messiah Lutheran Church–ELCA
Madison, Wisconsin

Tommy and Marvin were planting seeds in a small garden the city had set aside in the park for children to grow vegetables, when they heard a couple of men arguing about when the world would come to an end. "Do you think the world is coming to an end?" Marvin asked Tommy.

"I don't know," Tommy replied. "I never really think about it very much."

"One of the men talking over there said that he read in the Bible that the world would come to an end. Have you read that in the Bible?" Marvin asked.

"I guess the Bible does talk about it," Tommy said. "But not very much. It seems to me that if it were so important, as those two men seem to think, the Bible would say a lot more."

"I think so too," Marvin said. "In fact, if I thought the world was going to end tomorrow, I'd keep right on planting this garden."

Tommy started to laugh, and when Marvin asked him why he was laughing, Tommy told him that once Martin Luther was asked what he would do if he knew the world was going to end tomorrow, and he said he would plant a tree. "You sounded just like Martin Luther." And Tommy laughed again.

Tommy and his sister, Lindsay, were walking home from Sunday school when they walked across a little bridge over a stream. It reminded Lindsay of John the Baptist baptizing people in the River Jordan. "Were you baptized in a river?" she asked Tommy.

"I don't think so, but I really don't remember. Mom told me I was only a month old. Why do you want to know?

"Mom told me I was baptized in church at the baptismal font, and I was wondering if it made any difference how you were baptized. Are there different kinds of baptism?" Lindsay asked.

"I think so," Tommy said. "The Bible says John's baptism was a baptism of repentance. He was preparing people to get ready for the coming of Jesus. He wanted them to turn away from their sins and prepare for a new life following Jesus. When you and I were baptized, we were too young to repent. Dad told me that our baptism is God's way of telling us, and the world, that we are children of God and that God wants our parents and sponsors to teach us about Jesus and God—and that God loves us even more than our parents do."

"Wow, all that just from splashing a little water on us!" Lindsay was amazed.

"So it really doesn't matter how we are baptized," Tommy went on. "What matters is that we always remember we are children of God, which should make a difference in how we think and how we live."

Tommy and Marvin were talking about one of their favorite football players, who had just been caught using muscle-building drugs. "He used to be my hero; I always wanted to be just like him," Marvin said.

"Yeah, you really can't believe in anyone anymore," Tommy said.

"Not so, my friend," Marvin replied. "You can always believe in Jesus."

"Can we?" Tommy asked. "The Bible says even John the Baptist had questions about Jesus. I guess John thought Jesus' lifestyle was so different from his own that he wondered if he really was the Messiah."

"I remember that story," Marvin said. "John lived a very simple life out in the desert, and he thought Jesus was kind of a party guy, enjoying good food and good company. And I also remember what Jesus said: 'Listen to what I say, watch what I do, and then decide if I'm the Messiah.' That's why I believe in Jesus. He talked about loving and caring for one another. And the stories in the Bible show that he really did love and care about others, even his enemies."

"That's what I like about you, Marvin. Of all my friends, you are the most loving and caring friend I have. You really try to be a faithful follower of Jesus. So if I'm going to have a hero, somebody I can try to be like, it's going to be Jesus."

It was almost Christmas, and Tommy and his sister, Lindsay, were so excited, they could hardly stop talking about all the wonderful things they had put on their Christmas lists. Tommy's dad smiled at their happiness, but he was worried that they were missing the real point of Christmas.

"Tommy, Lindsay, come here. I want to tell you a story." Tommy and Lindsay loved it when their father told them a story, and so they ran over to his chair. He began, "You know the reason why we celebrate Christmas, don't you?" Of course they did, and they were a little embarrassed that they hadn't said much about the birth of Jesus.

Their father continued, "Jesus wasn't an ordinary man. He grew up to be the wisest and most caring man the world has ever known. He taught his followers a new way of living and made sure they knew that God loved them like a loving father, just like I love you, only even more. After his death, his followers told the many stories about his life over and over, and eventually these stories were written down so that they would always remember them.

"One of the stories was about his birth. Even Jesus's birth was special. He began to grow in Mary's womb in a very special way. He was truly a child of God, a gift from God. And so on December 25, we celebrate his birth. The Church wasn't sure when he was born, so they chose a time of great importance to almost everyone in the world at that time. During the month of December, the days kept getting shorter and shorter. It seemed like the sun was going away. But then on December 25, they began to notice that the days were getting longer; the sun wasn't going to disappear.

"Of course, today we know why the days get shorter and longer, but for the followers of Jesus, the gift of Jesus was the greatest gift of all; and so we celebrate it on what was then the greatest day of all. And because of that gift to us, we give gifts to those we love on Christmas."

Tommy went upstairs to call his sister for dinner. When he looked in her room, Lindsay was standing in front of the mirror, dressed in a robe with a scarf over her head.

"What are you doing, Lindsay?" Tommy asked.

"I'm practicing to be Mary in the Christmas pageant. And maybe you can be Joseph."

"They haven't even had the tryouts yet. And if you're Mary, then I think I'd like to be the innkeeper. 'Sorry, sister. There's no room in the inn. You'll have to go sleep in the barn.'"

"You know what, Tommy? I never thought about Jesus being born in a barn. In the Christmas pageant, we always see the manger in a beautiful church surrounded by angels and adoring shepherds. That's a terrible place for someone as special as Jesus to be born. Just think … the son of God's first bed was an animal feedbox."

"But remember," Tommy said. "Our pastor told us that when Jesus lived on earth, he was *true* man. That means he was just like you and me. We know he didn't have a lot of money and he wasn't powerful, but he did have a very special connection to God."

"Oh, Tommy," Lindsay said. "Do you think we could have that same kind of connection to God? I mean if Jesus was a true man, then we should be able to do what Jesus did."

"I know that's the way Jesus wanted his disciples to live. At first, they were called 'Followers of the Way'; Jesus even taught them to talk to God like God was their daddy."

"And," Lindsay said, "I think that at Christmas, we should celebrate Jesus as God's gift to us, to teach how to live connected to God. Jesus is God's Christmas present to us."

"And I think we better get downstairs for dinner before dad comes up to get us."

Tommy, Marvin and Danny were walking to school one morning when Tommy said, "Boy, I sure hope nothing bad happens today, I had a terrible nightmare last night."

"What did you have to eat before you went to sleep last night? Danny asked. "A couple of pieces of leftover pizza," Tommy said. "Do you think my dreams were the result of what I ate?"

Danny thought that might be the case, but Marvin wasn't so sure. "My dad said that a lot of times when he's working on a problem at work he'll dream about it at night and come up with a solution. In fact, dad always keeps a note pad beside his bed so he can jot things down while he still remembers them."

"Yeah," Tommy said, "It's like another part of our brain makes connections we couldn't make when we were awake."

Marvin began to think about his dreams. "Do you think God is trying to talk to us through our dreams? Just think about the stories in the Bible, like when Joseph was told to not be afraid to take Mary as his wife and then after Jesus was born, Joseph dreams that they need to go to Egypt and hide from the wicked king Herod."

"Wow! Tommy said, "Maybe we should pay more attention to the things we dream about." Do you think God was trying to tell me something last night?"

"You know," Danny said, "I kind 'a think Marvin's right. We should pay more attention to our dreams. But last night? I still think it was the pizza."

Tommy and his sister, Lindsay, were washing the dishes after dinner. It wasn't a job he liked to do, but he had no choice if he wanted to get his allowance.

"Why don't you do the dishes by yourself?" Tommy asked his sister. "I'm sure it will make God happy."

"How would God know? Are you going to tell God?"

"God is everywhere, and God knows everything," Tommy said

"How can somebody be everywhere?" Lindsay asked.

"God isn't somebody like you or me," Tommy said. "God doesn't have a body. God is a creative force so amazing that God is beyond our imagination. Just think about it: our universe is billions and billions of miles across; our solar system is only one of thousands of solar systems. And God is present in every one of them!"

"Wow, I never really thought about it. So if God is so great, how come God cares about who is doing the dishes? Or for that matter, how can God even care about me?" Lindsay was clearly disturbed by what Tommy had said.

"That, my dear sister, is what Christmas is all about. God came into the world in the person of Jesus to tell us that even as great as God is, God cares about each and every one of us. God even cares about the little birds, so you can be sure God cares about you. It's what the pastor called the *Incarnation*. God made it possible for us to see what God was like through the eyes of Jesus."

"So that means that even as great as God is, God still is able to watch over me and hear my prayers?" Lindsay was much relieved.

"Better than that," Tommy said. "When you pray, God wants you to talk to God like you were talking to someone as loving and close to you as your daddy."

Tommy and his friend Marvin were looking at the Christmas scene that was under the Christmas tree. It was the sixth of January, and the needles were beginning to fall, and of course the presents that had filled up the space were long ago opened and put away. Only the manger scene was left.

"Mom said she's going to take down the tree and put away the manger scene after Epiphany. I guess that's today," Tommy said.

"What is Epiphany, anyway?" Marvin asked.

"I think it's the church's celebration of the visit of the wise men. Mom said it used to be as important as Christmas, and in many places, it still is the time to exchange gifts. But we don't even have church services here unless the sixth happens to be a Sunday."

"You mean the wise men didn't visit the baby Jesus on his birthday?" Marvin was puzzled.

"Not unless it was his first birthday," Tommy replied. "Remember, in the Bible, it says they came from a long distance away. In fact, it was so far away it could have taken a year for them to get there."

"But look at this manger scene. There are the three wise men and even a camel. Why would they be included in the scene if they weren't even there?" Marvin asked.

"Well," Tommy said, feeling pretty smart because he had only that week asked his dad the same question and he knew the answer. "The wise men were an important part of the story. You see, the wise men came from the East, and they were not Jews. It was important to show us that Jesus wasn't only the savior of the Jewish people; Jesus was the savior of the whole world."

Tommy had gone over to Marvin's house to help him shovel the snow off his sidewalk. When they finished there, they went over to Tommy's house to shovel his walks. On their way there, Tommy said, "You know, Marvin, you are my very best friend."

Marvin felt the same way about Tommy and told him so. Then he said, "I was just thinking about the sermon on Sunday. Do you think John the Baptist and Jesus were good friends?"

"They could have been," Tommy replied. "After all, they were cousins, and they probably lived no more than twenty miles apart in Galilee. Although that was a good day's walk in Jesus's day. I think they got together on special occasions, like Passover and birthdays."

"What do you think it would be like to have been a friend of Jesus'?" Marvin asked.

"Marvin, you asked the weirdest questions." Tommy laughed. "But now that you mention it, in a way, Jesus is our friend. Isn't that what our baptism is all about? When we are baptized, it means that we are children of God, and our parents and godparents promise to teach us about Jesus so that we will always have Jesus as our guide and supporter. When you think about it, we know Jesus even better than John the Baptist did."

"And when did you become my Sunday school teacher?" Marvin was laughing too because this little talk had gone much deeper than he had intended. "But you're probably right. I just remembered that song we sang at church just a couple of weeks ago, 'What a Friend We Have in Jesus.' That's a different way of thinking about Jesus, but I really like it."

One day Tommy's dad came in the house to tell Tommy that a hummingbird was building a nest in a pot hanger they had left hanging from the roof of their covered patio entrance. Tommy's dad then took a small video camera and mounted it so they could watch the activity of the birds on their big screen TV in the family room.

First, they watched the two hummingbirds building a nest of mud and twigs. Then they plucked down from themselves to make the nest soft and comfy.

Tommy invited his friend Marvin to come and watch. It wasn't long before the mother bird laid three eggs in the nest. Both the mother and father took turns lying on the eggs to keep them warm, and in a few weeks, three little birds appeared.

Marvin and Tommy were amazed and watched the video as often as they could. One day, Marvin said, "Wouldn't it be nice if we would have had a video camera in Jesus's day so we could see Jesus as he lived with the disciples?"

Tommy, in one of his wiser moments, said, "Well, we kind of do. The disciples told the stories of what they saw over and over—so often that people memorized them. Then, quite a few years later, other followers wrote the stories down, and so today we can see Jesus through the stories in the four Gospels."

"I guess you're right," Marvin said. "But I still wish I could see a real live video."

Fortunately for us, several very good movies have been made. Perhaps the best is a TV series called *Jesus of Nazareth*. Another good film is simply called *Jesus*. Two other musical plays were turned into movies, *Godspell* and *Jesus Christ Superstar*. As with all movies and plays, things are added and left out and maybe given different kinds of interpretation, so you need to watch with a critical mind. But all of them can be used to help us see Jesus.

Pastor Girl

Tommy was on a camping trip with his Boy Scout troop. Tommy loved to go camping. He loved the smell of pine trees in the woods, he loved paddling his canoe around the lake, and he loved singing songs around the campfire at night.

On their first night in camp, they were sitting around the campfire on short logs that had been cut for firewood, roasting marshmallows for s'mores, and singing Tommy's favorite camp songs. All of a sudden, there was a flash of lightning. Seconds later, a loud clap of thunder was followed by a downpour of rain that felt like someone had dumped a bucket of water on them. The boys jumped from their logs and ran for their tents, not even stopping to put out the fire, although the heavy rain took care of that for them.

Fortunately, being good Scouts, they had built a trench around their tents, and once inside, they were warm and dry. Tommy put his wet clothes at the foot of his sleeping bag, crawled in, and fell sound asleep.

During the night, Tommy woke up and had to go to the bathroom. He felt around for his flashlight but he must have kicked it somewhere in their hurry to get out of the rain. He didn't want to wake up his partner, and he thought he remembered where the latrine was, so he headed out without a light. The rain had stopped, but it was totally black as he made his way across the campground.

Suddenly he tripped and fell right into a puddle of water. On the way back to his tent, the same thing happened. Tommy was a mess!

The next morning, he could see that when they jumped up from their logs, the logs went rolling and some had rolled onto the pathway. There was no way Tommy could have seen what he was stumbling over. In the same way, we stumble in our lives because we don't see the dangers or problems we face. Jesus is our light. He helps us see and avoid the dangers and problems.

Tommy and his family were on a vacation trip to visit his grandmother in Pennsylvania. They were driving down a country road when they came up behind a horse and buggy. Because it was a winding and hilly road, they had to drive very slowly behind it.

Tommy became impatient. "What is that?" he asked.

"It's a horse-drawn carriage." His father said, "The Amish people believe it's wrong to own automobiles, and so they drive carriages."

"What's wrong with driving a car?" Tommy wanted to know. "If they had a car, they wouldn't be holding us up."

"They don't have a problem with driving the car. It's owning it that they believe can become a problem. You see, Tommy, they think that some people have cars and a lot of other stuff just to show off, and they don't want to be guilty of pride and arrogance. So they live a life without a lot of *things.*"

"Like what?" Tommy asked

"Like curtains on the windows and electricity and TV."

"No TV?! I could never be an Amish person; I just couldn't live without a car or television."

"Not so fast," Tommy's dad said. "You really could live without them. And if you're honest, you'll have to admit there are a lot of things we think we need but are really just things we want. The Amish people help me to ask the question, 'What does it mean to be a follower of Jesus in this modern world?' From the sermon on the mount, I know that following Jesus may ask us to live differently from the rest of the world. How do you think Jesus wants you to live?"

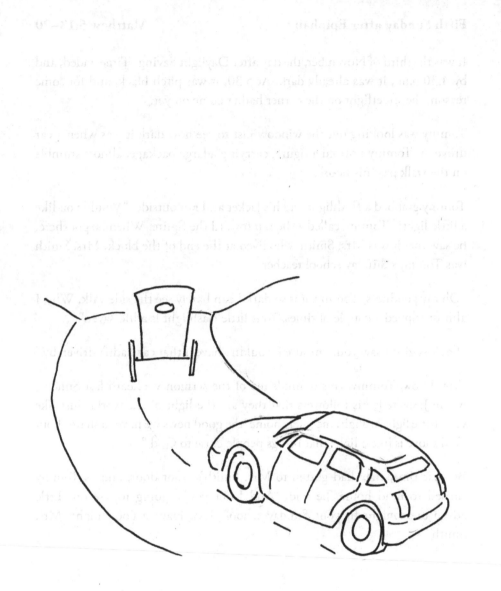

It was the third of November, the day after Daylight Savings Time ended, and by 4:30 p.m., it was already dark. At 5:30, it was pitch black, and for some reason, the streetlight on the corner hadn't come on yet.

Tommy was looking out the window just to see how dark it was when a car drove by. Tommy noticed a figure, carrying a large package, almost stumble on the walk past his house.

Tommy grabbed a flashlight and his jacket and ran outside. "Would you like a little light?" Tommy called as he ran toward the figure. When he got there, he saw that it was Mrs. Smith, who lived at the end of the block. Mrs. Smith was Tommy's Sunday school teacher.

"Oh my goodness, Tommy, it is so dark I can barely see the sidewalk. Why, I almost tripped a couple of times. Your little flashlight is a life-saver."

"I'm just glad I saw you. I'm sure I wouldn't have if that car hadn't driven by."

"You know, Tommy, this reminds me of the sermon we heard last Sunday, where Jesus tells his followers that they are the light of the world. Just like your little light brought me safely home, the good news we have to share about God's love is like a light that brings people close to God."

By that time, they had gotten to Mrs. Smith's front door, and as Tommy turned to head home, he said, "And I bet you're going to use our little adventure tonight in your Sunday school class. Have a good night, Mrs. Smith."

It had started snowing right after morning recess. It was one of those February snows that are heavy and wet, perfect for making snowballs. On the way home from school, Tommy saw his sister, Lindsay, walking up ahead. He thought he'd throw a snowball at her; if he threw it hard enough, it would land right at her feet.

But Tommy had a much stronger arm than he thought, and the snowball exploded right on the back of her head. And since she wasn't dressed for snow, the icy, wet snow went down her neck. Tommy jumped behind a bush, but Lindsay turned quickly and recognized the jacket of the boy who was trying to hide. It was her brother, Tommy!

That night, Lindsay didn't tell her parents what Tommy had done, but she never spoke a word to Tommy either. As they were headed upstairs for bed, she turned to Tommy and said, "That was a terrible thing you did, Tommy, and I am so mad at you, I'm never going to speak to you again."

"I'm really sorry," Tommy said. "I didn't mean for the snowball to hit you in the head. I didn't think I could throw it that far."

Lindsay wasn't about to forgive Tommy. She turned and gave him a shove, and Tommy went tumbling down the stairs. Luckily they weren't too far up the stairs, and Tommy wasn't hurt badly, but it hurt enough that he let out a yelp and started to cry. Lindsay was also crying because she was afraid she had broken Tommy's arm or something bad, and Tommy's mother came running to see what all the crying was about.

Between sobs, Tommy and Lindsay explained the whole story, from the snowball to the tumble. After listening to their story, their mother said, "I guess I have just one thing to add to the lesson you learned today. In the first place, we should never do things that may hurt someone, either by our words or our actions, and secondly, and perhaps most important, we should always be ready to forgive when someone says they're sorry."

Tommy was complaining to his friend Danny about Jack, the class bully. "Do you know what he did during lunch today? He stuck out his foot and tripped me when I was carrying my lunch, and I spilled it all over the floor, and everyone laughed at me. Boy, would I like to get even with him."

Danny's response wasn't what Tommy expected. "Sure, you can probably think of a way to get even, and then Jack will think of something even worse to do to you, and it will just keep on going. Why don't you try doing what Jesus said?"

"I don't think Jesus had to deal with someone like Jack. What did he say anyway?"

"You know," Danny said. "Jesus said we should love our enemies and do good to those who would hurt us."

"I don't know," Tommy objected. "It sounds nice, but I don't think it will work."

"I thought you believed Jesus. You won't know until you try it."

So Tommy did. The next day he offered Jack one of his mother's homemade cupcakes, but Jack said he wouldn't eat any garbage Tommy brought. The next day Tommy offered Jack his extra Aaron Rogers football card. Jack took the card but told Tommy he was still on his bad list. The next day, Tommy was cleaning the blackboard for his teacher when he overheard the teacher telling Jack he better do a good job on the test tomorrow or he might have to repeat third grade.

At suppertime, Tommy called Jack and asked him if he would like to study for the exam with Danny and himself. He pointed out that Danny was really smart, and Jack took him up on his offer. The next day Jack did better on the test than he had ever done before, and from that day on, Jack and Tommy were friends.

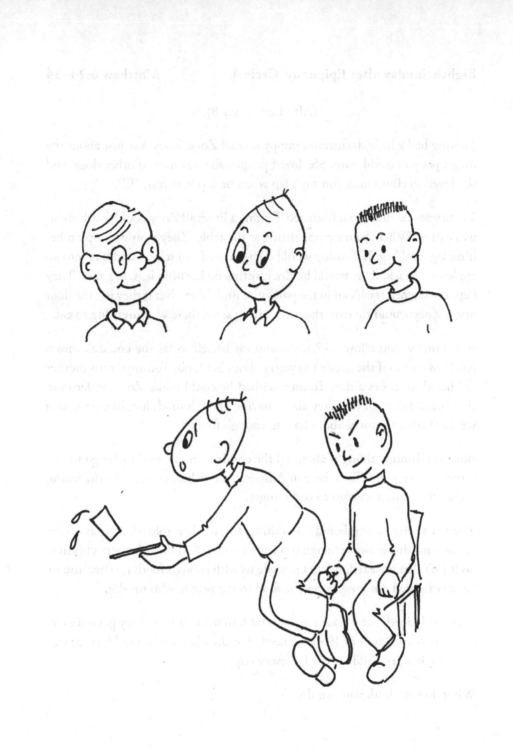

(Also Lectionary 8)

Tommy had a little dachshund puppy named Zoey. Zoey was just about the nicest pet you could have. She loved people, she was nice to other dogs, and she loved to climb into Tommy's lap when he was watching TV.

There was one thing that bothered Tommy a little: all Zoey could think about was eating. When Tommy was sitting at the table, Zoey would sit up on her hind legs and beg. If Tommy would come home from school and bite into an apple for a snack, there would be Zoey, sitting on her hind legs, begging. They kept the kitchen trash can in the pantry behind a door, but if they left the door open, Zoey would tip over the trash can to see if there was anything to eat.

If Tommy would allow it, Zoey would eat herself so fat she couldn't move. And it wasn't as if she needed to worry about her food. Tommy or his mother fed her three times a day. Tommy wished he could make Zoey understand that she didn't need to worry about having enough food, just like Jesus said we don't need to worry about having enough food.

But then Tommy thought about all the children in the world who go to bed hungry every night. Even here in America, the richest country in the world, there are children who go to bed hungry.

Then Tommy remembered something his teacher told their class. Our restaurants throw away enough food every day to feed those hungry children. So it isn't that the earth doesn't provide us with enough food; it is because we haven't figured out how to get the food to the people who need it.

Tommy decided that it wasn't enough for him to make sure Zoey got fed every day, but as a follower of Jesus, he needed to do whatever he could to see that all those hungry children got fed every day.

What do you think you can do?

Transfiguration Sunday   **Matthew 17:1–9**

When Tommy's dad was asked to move to Long Beach, California, for a few years to help start a branch of his company, Tommy became good friends with Peter, his pastor's son. Peter had leukemia and was in remission when he shared this story with Tommy,

It was early Sunday morning, and Peter and his father were driving to church to get ready for Peter's confirmation. It hadn't rained for months, but all of a sudden it started to rain.

"I'm glad it's raining," Peter said.

Peter's father was puzzled. "Why would you want it to rain on your Confirmation Day?"

"Because," Peter explained, "I prayed that if God was really there, he would make it rain on my Confirmation Day."

Peter's father shook his head. "That's really bad theology, Peter. In the first place, we should never put God to the test, and secondly, I don't think God messes around with the weather because we want him to."

"I know, Dad, but living with Leukemia and knowing that it could come back any day and take away my life is scary. Sometimes you need a mountaintop experience to let you know that God is there. It's like when Jesus took Peter, James, and John up on the mountain and was transfigured before he was crucified. It was a special experience of God that helped them through the tough days ahead."

It may have just been a coincidence, but that rain on his Confirmation Day did give Peter the strength he needed when the leukemia did come back and take his life.

When Tommy's friend, Marvin, moved to Tommy's town, he was the only African American in their school. Most of the kids were just fine with that, but a few of them did not like people who looked different. It was something they probably learned at home.

One day when Tommy and Marvin were walking together, a couple of boys started teasing them and using the "N" word. It is a very hurtful word some people use to refer to African Americans. To make matters worse, both the boys belonged to the same church as Tommy.

This time, Tommy walked over to the boys and looked them in the eyes and said, "You should be ashamed of yourselves. You are acting like bullies. And worse than that, you should know that a follower of Jesus doesn't act like that."

When Tommy went back to where Marvin was, Marvin was really surprised. "Wow! You really took those guys on. But how come you laid a Jesus trip on them? I thought you didn't like to make a public showing of your faith."

"Whatever gave you that idea?" Tommy asked

"Remember when that Carter kid would drop to one knee and bow his head after he scored a touchdown? You sure didn't think much of that display of his faith."

"That's totally different," Tommy said. "What Carter was doing was almost like boasting, 'See what a fine Christian I am?' And it also makes it look like he thinks God is on his side. I really don't think God takes sides at a football game.

"But there are times when followers of Jesus have to stand up for what they believe. You shouldn't be ashamed of your faith or afraid to say what Jesus has told us is right."

Danny and Tommy were walking home from the Friday-night football game when Danny asked Tommy if he had seen the guy walking across Niagara Falls on a wire.

"Yeah," Tommy said. "That's something you could never tempt me to do."

"Of course not," Danny replied. "It wouldn't be a temptation for you. You know you couldn't even walk five feet on a wire. So for you to try would be certain death. That's not temptation; that's suicide.

"Now, see those guys up ahead smoking cigarettes? If they were to stop and offer you a cigarette, and you might think, *I wonder what it's like to smoke. It seems so grown up, and no one would ever know if I tried just one.* That's a temptation. Because you might try one, and then another and another, and pretty soon you're addicted. And then you die of lung cancer. A temptation is something that you think might be fun or even good for you, but it's really harmful and might even take your life."

"Oh, I see," Tommy said. "It's like when those kids try taking drugs and get hooked and then overdose; that's temptation. But in the Bible, it said that Jesus was tempted in the wilderness. How could Jesus be tempted if he was God and knew everything?"

"You forget," Danny replied, "the Bible also said Jesus gave up all his godly powers and became a true human. So those were very real temptations for Jesus. And there were probably other temptations, maybe like trying to run away and hide from being crucified."

"So if Jesus was a true human just like you and me, then we should try to be the same kind of human being he was."

"Well, I don't know if he was just like you and me, but you're beginning to get the point."

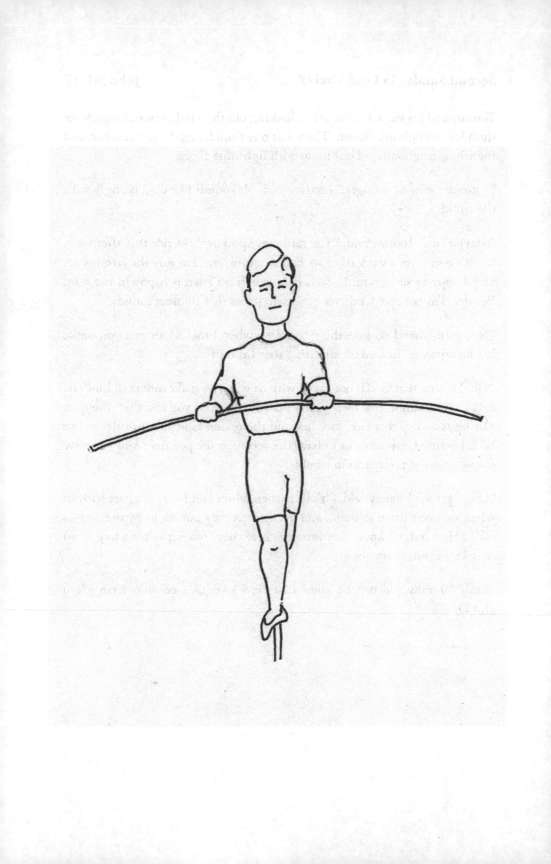

Tommy and his sister, Lindsay, were looking out the window, watching a huge thunder and lightning storm. There was one thunder crash after another, and the whole neighborhood was lit up with lightning flashes.

"Thunder sounds so angry," Lindsay said. "It sounds like God is angry with the world."

"Maybe not," Tommy said. "The rain may spoil my bike ride this afternoon, but it's been over a week since we had any rain, and I'm sure the farmers are very happy to see it rain. In fact, even our front lawn is happy in the rain. Besides, I'm not sure God ever gets as angry as that thunder sounds."

"Not even when I do something bad, like when I told Mom that you broke her favorite vase instead of admitting that I did it?"

"Oh, I'm sure that God is not happy with us when we make mistakes, Lindsay; and I have to admit that I was pretty mad at you when you told that whopper. But Jesus told us that God loves us, and the reason God gave us rules to live by is because God wants us to have the very best life possible. And when we screw up, we get ourselves in trouble."

"Oh, I get it," Lindsay said. "It's like when Mom and Dad are upset with us when we don't listen to them, and even when they punish us by making us take a time out, we know they love us 'cause they always give me a hug when they let me out of my room.

"And," Tommy added, "We know that God loves us even more than Mom and Dad!"

Tommy's sister, Lindsay, came into the house with tears running down her cheeks. Her mother heard her sobbing and hurried into the room. "What's wrong?" she asked.

"I was playing with Jessica, (sob) and I told her I was going to be a minister when I grow up, (sob) and she told me that I couldn't be a minister (sob) because God doesn't want women to be ministers. Is that true, Mommy?"

"No, honey, it's not. It is true that women are not allowed to be pastors in some churches, but they allow women to minister in other ways. In our church, however, women can serve as pastors, parish workers, parish nurses, teachers, and in any way that men are called to ministry.

"In fact, there's a wonderful little story in John's Gospel about a woman Jesus met at a well near the city of Sychar in the country of Samaria. Now it's important to know that the people of Samaria were at one time connected to the Jews, but in Jesus' day, they were not even friends, so the woman was surprised that Jesus would even talk to her.

"But not only did Jesus talk with her, he asked her to go into the city and invite her friends to come and listen to him telling about the coming of the Kingdom of God. This happened early in Jesus's ministry, so she may have been the very first evangelist. So you see, Jesus must have thought women were very capable of being ministers.

"So, Lindsay, God is delighted that you are thinking about being a minister, and by the way, so am I."

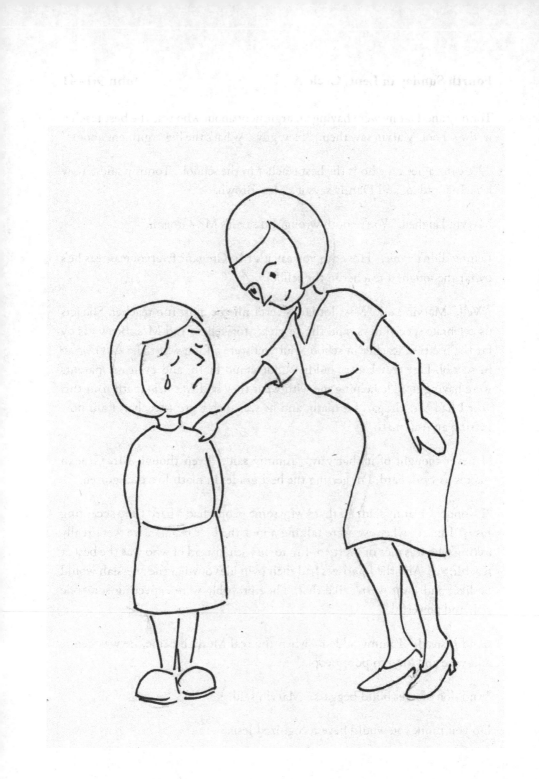

Tommy and Danny were having an argument about who was the best teacher in the school. Marvin saw them. "Hey, guys! What's the big argument about?"

"We can't agree on who is the best teacher in the school," Tommy said. "I say it's Miss Jordan, and Danny says it's Mrs. Brown."

Marvin laughed. "You're both wrong. I'd say it's Mr. Grogan."

Danny didn't agree. "How can you say it's Mr. Grogan? Everyone agrees he's by far the toughest teacher in the school."

"Well," Marvin said, "Miss Jordan is certainly the most fun teacher. She lets us celebrate special days, and she's a great storyteller. And Mrs. Brown is by far the prettiest teacher in school. But you were asking who's the *best teacher* in school. Last year I just couldn't understand math, and even my parents were having trouble helping me with what they said was *new* math. But this year I had Mr. Grogan for math, and he was such a great teacher, I am now getting an A in math."

"I never thought of it that way," Tommy said. "Even though Mr. Grogan makes us work hard, I'm getting the best grades in math I've ever gotten."

"I wonder," Danny said, "if that's why some people had a hard time accepting Jesus? I mean, when we were talking about the best teacher, we were really asking who was nice or pretty or fun to be with instead of who was the best at teaching us. And the Pharisees had their own idea of what the Messiah would be like, and Jesus wasn't like that. They probably were expecting someone rich and powerful."

"And instead," Tommy added, "when the real Messiah came, he was gentle and wise and kind to poor people."

"And don't forget blind beggars," Marvin said.

Do you think you would have recognized Jesus?

Tommy didn't like March very much. One day it could be sunny and almost 70 degrees, and the next day there would be ten inches of heavy, wet snow. Like last week. Tommy wore his spring jacket to school, and before recess, it started to snow. When school let out, there were already six inches on the ground and more coming down.

Usually, Mr. Adams would ask Tommy to shovel his walk, but Tommy was in school, and so Mr. Adams thought he'd shovel it before it got too deep. But it was already very heavy, and poor Mr. Adams collapsed. Someone called the ambulance, and just as Tommy was coming home, the medics were carrying Mr. Adams into the ambulance.

Tommy was very worried. Mr. Adams was a good friend. In addition to mowing his lawn and shoveling his walks, Tommy would also help him in the garden, and very often they would go fishing together. That night, Mrs. Adams called Tommy's mom to tell her that Mr. Adams had died. Tommy's mom had to tell Tommy the sad news.

"What happens to Mr. Adams now?" Tommy asked.

"Remember in the story of creation when God breathed into Adam?" she asked, and Tommy nodded. "Well, every human being has this breath of God. We call it our soul. Our bodies get old and wear out, but our souls are eternal; that means they don't die. Our souls return to God, who is the source of life."

"What do our souls do then?" Tommy asked.

Tommy's mom had a big smile. "That's a good question, Tommy, but no one really knows. What we do know is that we don't have to worry about it because Jesus told us we will be with him and no one will have any pain and there won't any crying anymore."

"That must be good news for Mrs. Adams," Tommy said.

His mother gave Tommy a big hug. "It's good news for all of us!"

Sunday of the Passion, Procession, Cycle A, B, C   Matthew 21:1–11

It was the Sunday before Easter, and on this Sunday, the congregation gathered outside the church in the fellowship hall. They used to gather outside in the parking lot, but last year it rained. This year, however, the sun was shining bright, although it was a little chilly outside.

Everyone received a long palm leaf, and they were waiting for the pastor to read the Palm Sunday lesson. Tommy was standing next to his friend, Danny. "I love parades," Tommy said.

"So do I," Danny replied. "I wonder what it would have been like to be in Jerusalem on that first Palm Sunday. Just think of the people singing and shouting, "Hosanna." They must have been so amazed and excited to see the great teacher, Jesus."

"But," Tommy said, "why do you think everything changed by Friday? Then the crowd was shouting, 'Crucify him, crucify him!' It must have been a different crowd."

What do you think happened between Sunday and Friday?

Do you think it was a different crowd?

As Tommy left church on Sunday, he shook the pastor's hand. "That was a very long Gospel reading this morning, Pastor."

"It sure was, Tommy," the pastor replied. "But for a very good reason."

"What was that?" Tommy asked.

"Well, Tommy, as we begin this most important week of all the celebrations in our church, it's important for us to listen to the entire biblical story of the events we are celebrating this week.

"On Thursday, we will hear about Jesus and his disciples celebrating the Passover, when Jesus teaches the disciples a new celebration: the Lord's Supper or communion, a time when we are assured of Jesus' presence in our lives.

"Then on Friday, we once again remember the sacrifice Jesus made out of love for his disciples of every age. We are reminded of God's amazing grace when Jesus forgives even those who were crucifying him.

"And on Sunday, we celebrate that death is not the final word, and we, like Jesus, will live forever with God. Really, Tommy, our whole faith is proclaimed in the events we celebrate this week: that we are connected to God, that we are forgiven and called to dedicate our lives to love and serve others, and that we do not need to be afraid because God is with us and death is not the end of our spirit.

"So that is why, on this very special Sunday, we take the time to listen to that painful but beautiful story of Jesus' sacrifice and love, knowing that next Sunday we celebrate the resurrection."

On the Thursday of Holy Week, the pastor asked Tommy if he would help in a drama about the night Jesus celebrated the Passover with his disciples. She wanted Tommy to come up in the chancel and read this statement:

"I represent all the poor children in the world, the children who are sick and have no medicine to make them well, the children who are hungry and have no food, the children who are alone and have no one to care for them. These are God's children, and we as followers of Jesus are called to provide medicine and food and comfort. Tonight you will wash my feet as a symbol of your answer to that call."

Then she asked Tommy to take off his shoes and socks, and she would wash his feet.

After the service, Tommy's sister, Lindsay, asked him how he felt having the pastor wash his feet.

"It really felt kind of weird," Tommy said. "It didn't seem right having the pastor wash my feet."

"Just think of how the disciples must have felt when Jesus took the role of a servant. I can understand why Peter didn't want Jesus to wash his feet."

"And remember," Tommy said, "Jesus asked his disciples to wash each other's feet. What that means is that the followers of Jesus are asked to serve the needs of all the poor and sick and hungry people. That's a really big job, but I think if all the followers of Jesus did just a little, together we could do it."

The Sunday before Good Friday, the children in Tommy's class were asked by their Sunday school teacher to share what the cross meant to them. This is what Tommy said:

"When I was baptized, my grandmother gave me a cross on a gold chain that had belonged to her grandmother. It was very old and precious, so my mother put it away in a safe place, but when I started first grade, my mother would let me wear it to church on Sundays.

"My cross is a beautiful piece of jewelry, but the cross is not a beautiful thing. The cross in Jesus's day was a thing of death—in fact, as horrible a death as the Romans could think of. It was designed to be a terrible punishment to make people afraid to break the law.

"By dying on a cross, Jesus showed that he was willing to suffer this horrible death in order to make known God's love and forgiveness for all people.

"When Jesus asked his disciples to take up their cross like he did, he was asking them, and all who would become his disciples, to be willing to give their lives so that others would know God's love.

"So my cross *is* beautiful because it reminds me of God's great love for me and also that I am asked to tell everyone about God's great love for them."

It was early Easter morning. Tommy and his sister, Lindsay, had just returned from the sunrise service in the park, and before they headed to church for the Easter breakfast, they stopped at home to hunt for Easter eggs.

Lindsay had just picked up a pink Easter egg and was turning it over in her hand. "What does the Easter bunny have to do with the story of Jesus's resurrection?" she asked.

"Good question," Tommy said. "And why isn't it the Easter chicken? After all, bunnies don't lay eggs."

"Don't be silly, Tommy. I'm serious. What does all this stuff about Easter eggs and bunnies have to do with the Easter story?"

"To be honest, I don't really know," Tommy said. "But I have some ideas. First of all, Easter is about new life, and Easter is also connected to the major Old Testament celebration, Passover, which was also a celebration of new life. *And,* both Easter and Passover are celebrated in the spring, and spring is a time of new life when the leaves begin to grow and the grass turns green."

"So," Lindsay said, "eggs are also the beginning of new life. But I still don't know where the bunny comes in."

"Neither do I," Tommy said. "But the important thing is new life. And remember the pastor's sermon this morning? He said that because God forgives us when we make mistakes, every day is like a new beginning for us. So today I wish you a happy new life."

"And a happy new life to you, Tommy."

Tommy and Marvin were walking home from Sunday school when Tommy asked Marvin, "Do you believe that miracles still happen today?"

"Sure," Marvin said.

"I mean like hungry people being fed and sick people being cured," replied Tommy.

"That's exactly what I mean," said Marvin. "Last year, our church raised over $15 million to feed thousands of hungry people all over the world, and out at University Hospital, hundreds of people have gotten new kidneys and livers and hearts."

"Those aren't miracles; they're things that have been done by smart people and good people who wanted to help." Tommy wasn't about to lose this argument.

"Well, what about the sunrise or this beautiful flower?" Marvin pressed on.

"Those aren't miracles either; they happen every day."

"I think they are miracles. After all, believing is seeing."

"No, you've got it wrong. It's, 'Seeing is believing.'"

"Maybe so," Marvin said, "but when you believe, you can see God at work in a hundred different ways every day. When you believe, you see the world differently. When you believe, you see miracles."

It was an election year, and while Tommy didn't pay much attention to the political debates, he did know who the president of the United States was and that he was stopping in Tommy's town on his way from one big city to another. The school let the students out early so they could go and see the president, and a lot of the kids used the time out of school for extra play time. But Tommy and his friends headed for the city park, where they had announced that the president's bus would stop.

The boys worked their way through the crowd and got next to the rope that had been set up to hold the crowd back. The bus came, and the president was the first one off. He immediately went over to where the boys were standing and began shaking hands. He even shook the outstretched hands of Danny, Marvin, and Tommy.

On the way home, Marvin was going on and on about what a great thing it was to see the president in person. "You know who I'd like to see?" Danny said. "I'd like to see Jesus."

"Me too," Tommy chimed in. "Like the disciples did after the resurrection. How about those disciples in the Gospel reading last Sunday. They spent half a day with Jesus and didn't even recognize him."

"Well," Marvin said, "you spend every Sunday morning with Jesus and apparently you don't recognize him either."

"What do you mean?" Danny asked.

"Don't you remember from our first communion class?" Marvin said. "The pastor told us that Jesus was truly present in the bread and wine. When we take communion, we are assured of Jesus's promise that he goes with us, even after we leave the church."

"You're right, Marvin," Danny said. "And I think that's the best part of taking communion."

Tommy was walking home from school with his best friends, Danny and Marvin, when one of the high school kids came up to him and asked, "Hey, kid, are you happy?"

"Yeah, I'm happy," Tommy replied.

"I mean really happy. I've got a pill here that'll make you feel like you're king of the world, and it'll only cost you five bucks."

"No thanks," Tommy said with what he hoped was enough emphasis so the kid would leave him alone. "And besides, I don't even have five bucks."

And with that, the kid walked away. Tommy turned to his friends. "Can you believe the nerve of that guy? Selling drugs right here on the street in broad daylight. I'm sure glad my dad talked to me about drugs. Do you know that if you start taking drugs, you can get addicted? That means you can't stop taking them even after you realize how bad they are for you."

"Yeah," Marvin added. "And sometimes you take too much and it kills you. Every day there's a story in the paper about someone dying from an overdose of drugs, my dad reads it to me so I'll be sure to know how bad they can be."

Danny, who the boys often kid about being their Bible teacher, added, "That kid reminds me of the Gospel reading on Sunday where Jesus talks about those who pretended to offer good things but really came to steal and kill. But Jesus shows us the way to the really good life."

What would you do if someone tried to sell you drugs?

It was a warm summer evening, and Tommy and his sister, Lindsay, were lying on the grass in the front yard, looking up at the stars. Tommy knew some of the constellations, and he was pointing them out to Lindsay.

"There's the Big Dipper and the Little Dipper, and there to the right is Orion."

"How many stars are there?" Lindsay asked

"Millions, maybe billions. I know we can't begin to see them all, not even all the ones in our own galaxy," Tommy replied.

"Where is heaven?" Lindsay asked another impossible question.

"I don't think anyone knows," Tommy said. "And before you ask another question I can't answer, I don't know what heaven looks like either."

"Then how do you know there is a heaven?" First graders just keep asking questions.

"I know because Jesus said that when we die, we are going to be with him. He doesn't say what heaven will be like; he doesn't even say what we will be like. He simply says that there is a place for us and that we will be with him and there will be no pain or suffering and it will be nice. And that's good enough for me."

And Lindsay, done with her questions, said, "That's good enough for me, too."

Just before going to bed, Tommy had watched the movie *Oliver Twist*, based on the book of the same name written by Charles Dickens. As he lay in bed, dozens of thoughts went flashing through his mind.

He thought about how sad it would be to be an orphan and how important it would be to get connected to a person or group of people who would care about you, not like the thieves who drew Oliver Twist into their gang.

He thought about how lucky he was to live in the family he enjoyed. His parents provided him with a nice home and everything he ever needed. And most important of all, they loved him. It felt so good to be loved! Even his little sister, who could sometimes be a pest, was loving in her own way.

And then he thought about kids who weren't orphans but who didn't have the same kind of home he had, homes where drugs and alcohol abuse caused child abuse.

And finally, as he thought about all the important connections in his life, he thought about his connection to God. Jesus said God's Spirit will be in him. Wherever he goes and whatever he is doing, God's Spirit is with him!

In his baptism, God said he was a child of God. And if he is a child of God, then all other people are children of God, and they too have God's Spirit in them. Most important, all those people are my brothers and sisters.

And with that thought, Tommy went to sleep, thinking how wonderful it was to be so connected.

Tommy lived in a small town in Wisconsin where everyone was pretty much like everyone else. In fact, they were almost all of German descent, with a few Norwegians thrown in. One Sunday, a new kid showed up at church. He was about the same size as Tommy, but he looked a little different. He had dark brown skin and black curly hair. Tommy wasn't sure if he could be friends with someone who looked so different, but he had just had a Sunday school lesson about Jesus loving everybody, so he thought he would give it a try.

"What's your name?" Tommy asked.

"Marvin," Marvin replied.

"How come you look different than me?" Tommy asked again.

"Because I'm African American, like most of the professional basketball players. We African Americans have dark skin and curly hair, but otherwise, I'm pretty much just like you. I even belong to the same kind of church you go to."

At that, Tommy smiled and he said, "My name is Tommy, and I'd like to be your friend." And so they became best friends. Pretty soon Marvin became friends with all of Tommy's friends, and he felt right at home in Tommy's church.

It wasn't long after that, that Tommy's church sponsored a refugee family from Vietnam. They had a boy about Tommy's age, and he looked a little different too. But that no longer mattered because Tommy and Marvin knew that inside, they were all pretty much alike. Then a family moved into town that had a son with Muscular Dystrophy who had to use a wheelchair to get around, and he also became a part of the group at church.

One Sunday after church, Tommy's mom took a picture of Tommy and his friends, and when his mother printed the picture and showed it to Tommy, Tommy said, "Hey, that looks just like the picture of God's family in our Sunday school lesson."

Today we have adult crossing guards at the major crosswalks where children cross the street to get to school, but when Tommy was in school, they had patrol boys and patrol girls. They were chosen from the best students in the school, and they got to wear a white band around their waists and across their shoulders. Their job was to keep the children at the curb until they went out in the street and made sure they could get across the street safely.

The day before classes started, all the patrol boys and girls came to school to receive their belts and their instructions on how to do their jobs. I think Tommy was a little too taken with his new power.

As Tommy and his friends were walking home from the meeting, Tommy said, "Boy oh boy, with this belt I get to say who can go to school and who can't."

"Wait a minute," Marvin said. "You get to say *when* they can cross the street."

"But our job is to see to it that they all get across the street safely," Danny chimed in. "If we weren't there, they might get hit by a car trying to get to school."

"I know what our job is," Tommy chuckled. "I just didn't say it right. Of course every kid is supposed to be in school, and we are appointed to see that they get there safely."

"It's like when Jesus gave the disciples the keys of the kingdom," Danny went on. "The disciples weren't given the power to decide who gets into the kingdom; they were given the responsibility to tell everyone about God's love and forgiveness."

Tommy couldn't wait to be eleven years old because then he would be old enough to be a Boy Scout. He had been a Cub Scout for three years, and he had earned all his badges. When he turned eleven, he could be a Boy Scout.

On his birthday, he couldn't wait to open his present from his parents because he was pretty sure what it would be. Sure enough, when he opened it, there was a brand new Boy Scout uniform just his size. He immediately ran to his room and came back to the party dressed in his new uniform.

"At last, I'm a Boy Scout," Tommy declared.

"Not so fast, Tommy." It was Marvin, who was two months older than Tommy and was already a Boy Scout. "There are a number of things you have to *do* before you become a Tenderfoot, and until then, you aren't really a Boy Scout."

"Like what?" Tommy Asked.

"Well, for one thing, you need to know the Scout oath, law, motto, and slogan."

"I learned all those in Cub Scouts."

"And then you have to demonstrate your ability in tying knots and taking physical activities and knowledge of the rules for safe hiking. There's a lot more to being a Scout than wearing the uniform."

"Marvin's right." Tommy's dad joined the conversation. "It's a lot like being a Christian. It's important to believe that Jesus is your Lord and Savior, but it's also important to learn about the way Jesus taught us to live. When Jesus gave the disciples their commission, he told them to baptize *and* to teach others to live as Jesus taught them."

Tommy and his family were on vacation at an oceanside resort in Florida. Tommy loved going to the ocean, especially in Florida, where the water was always warm and there were beautiful sandy beaches.

Tommy was busy building a sand castle. He had been working on it ever since lunch. It was a huge castle, with six-inch-high walls and twelve ten-inch-high towers. But as Tommy was busily working on his castle, he didn't notice that the tide was rising, until …

All at once, a large wave came in, splashed over his castle, and ran down the beach, back into the ocean. The castle was nothing but a little mound of sand. "Hey, Mom," Tommy said, "it's just like that song we learned in Sunday school." And Tommy began to sing the song.

The wise man built his house upon a rock,
    The wise man built his house upon a rock,
The wise man built his house upon a rock,
    And the rains came tumbling down.

The rains came down, and the floods came up,
    The rains came down, and the floods came up,
The rains came down, and the floods came up,
    And the wise man's house stood firm.

The foolish man built his house upon the sand,
    The foolish man built his house upon the sand,
The foolish man built his house upon the sand,
    And the rains came tumbling down.

The rains came down, and the floods came up,
    The rains came down, and the floods came up,
The rains came down, and the floods came up
    And the foolish man's house went plop.

So build your house on the Lord, Jesus Christ,
    So build your house on the Lord, Jesus Christ,
So build your house on the Lord, Jesus Christ,
    And the building will stand firm.

George had been away for over a year when one day he showed up at school. It didn't take long for word to get around that George had been sent to reform school for stealing his neighbor's car. Reform school is where they send young people instead of jail in an attempt to change their lives for the better. At lunchtime, Tommy saw his friend, Danny, sitting at a table with George and eating lunch with him.

After lunch, Tommy asked Danny if he knew that George had just gotten out of jail. "Of course I know," Danny said. "Everybody in school seems to know."

"Then why would you be seen eating lunch with him?" Tommy asked.

Danny was surprised that his good friend Tommy would even ask such a question. All he could say was, "Why not?"

"Well," Tommy said, "he's not a very nice person. He's a criminal. I wouldn't want a criminal for a friend."

"How would you know what kind of a person he is? You haven't even talked to him. I found him to be a very nice person. Sure, he made a mistake, a big one, but now he wants a new beginning. George never wants to go back to jail, and he needs good people who will be friends with him.

"And besides," Danny continued, "don't you remember the story in Matthew's Gospel? Matthew would never have become a disciple if Jesus hadn't reached out to him. The Pharisees were just like you. They questioned what kind of a person Jesus was when he made friends with people they thought weren't very nice, but Jesus said he came especially to help those people start a new life."

"You're right, Danny. I just wasn't thinking the way Jesus thinks. In fact, if it's okay with you, I'd like to join you and George for lunch tomorrow."

And that's what Tommy did, and he also invited Marvin to join them, and they all became best friends.

Tommy and his friends Marvin, Danny, and George got together with eight of their friends to form a baseball team for Little League. There was going to be a meeting at school on Tuesday night to sign up and start planning for the new season. At the end of the meeting, the leader came over to Tommy and his friends.

"I'm sorry, boys, but we don't have a coach for your team, and without a coach, your team won't be able to play in Little League. Maybe one of your dads would be able to coach."

So the boys went home and each one asked his dad if he would coach their team; and each one said he was just too busy and wouldn't be able to coach. Some of them said they might be able to coach next year ... but that didn't help solve the problem this year.

Tommy said, "I know what to do. Let's ask our pastor if she could help us find a coach." So they went and asked their pastor. It turned out she also was too busy, but she did make an announcement after church asking anyone who was willing to help to give her a call.

On Sunday evening, the pastor called Tommy to tell him she had found a coach for their team. "You know, Tommy," she said, "your search for a coach reminds me of the Gospel reading this morning. You boys looked so sad and lost when you came to me to ask for help finding a coach, just like the people in our Gospel reading who were helpless like sheep without a shepherd. People need to hear the good news that God loves them and wants what is best for them. But just like your team can't play without a coach, they won't hear the good news without someone to tell them." And then she asked Tommy a question that he thinks about almost every day.

"Have you thought about being a pastor? I think you would be really good at sharing the good news; but remember, even if you don't become a pastor, God still wants you to tell others about Jesus."

Tommy and his sister, Lindsay, didn't fight very often, but when they did, it was usually because Tommy wanted things to go his way. On this occasion, they were fighting about who could choose the TV program at 7:00 this evening. Tommy wanted to watch a comedy, and Lindsay wanted to watch a reality show.

Since Tommy was older, he usually got his way, and that's exactly what happened on this day. Lindsay was upset. "You always get your way, Tommy. You are so self-centered." And then, for extra emphasis, she thought she'd throw in the Bible for added support. "You are just the kind of person Jesus warned about in the Gospel reading last Sunday."

That last statement bothered Tommy because he thought he was a follower of Jesus, and for Lindsay to suggest that he wasn't, or at least wasn't a *good* follower, just didn't seem fair. "Oh yeah?" Tommy replied. "And just what do you think Jesus said that applies to me?"

"When Jesus said, 'Whoever seeks to save their life will lose it and whoever loses their life for my sake will find it.' The pastor told us Jesus was saying that those who seek to save their lives are people who are self-centered, who think only about themselves, and those who lose their lives are people who think about others before they think of themselves. So it seems to me you are in the group that loses their lives."

For once Tommy realized that his little sister was right. "You know, Lindsay, you made a good point. I guess I wasn't listening very well when the pastor said that. How about if we take turns picking what to watch on TV? Tonight it's your turn."

Tommy and Marvin stopped by Tommy's house on the way home from school. "Hi, Mom," Tommy said. "Is it all right if Marvin stays here for a while? We have a homework assignment that we are supposed to work on together."

"Of course Tommy, would you like me to get you some milk and cookies?"

"That would be great, Mom. Do you want us to come to the kitchen?"

"No, I'll bring them down to your room."

As they walked down the hall to Tommy's room, Marvin said, "I really like coming to your house, Tommy. Your mom always offers us something to eat, and best of all, she doesn't stay around and watch us like she's afraid we're going to break something."

"I asked Mom about that, and she said it's called *hospitality*."

"Hospitality? What's hospitality?" Marvin asked. "I know our pastor talked about hospitality at our church, but I don't know what it means."

"Mom explained it this way. She said it means making your guests feel comfortable by seeing if there is anything they need and at the same time giving them the freedom to be themselves."

"What does 'freedom to be themselves' mean?" Marvin asked.

"Mom says it means making them feel welcome just the way they are: the way they dress, their race, the way they cut their hair, even the way they think about politics and all that kind of stuff."

"Now I get it. Hospitality at church means telling the visitors where things are, like the restroom, and helping them with the bulletin and hymnal and not fussing about how they're dressed—even letting them sit where you usually sit."

"Yep," Tommy said. "That's hospitality."

Danny and Tommy usually walked home from school together, but today Danny started walking home without waiting for Tommy. When Tommy saw Danny walking about a block ahead, he was pretty sure he knew why, and he ran to catch up with him.

"Hey, Danny, wait up," Tommy called. Danny just kept walking and didn't respond. Tommy finally caught up with Danny. "I'm really sorry," Tommy blurted out.

"Well you should be." There was just a little anger in Danny's reply. "You were standing right next to me when those guys cornered me and started calling me 'four eyes' and 'geeky' and making fun of my books. And what did you do?"

Tommy's chin was down on his chest, and he mumbled, "I walked away."

"That's right. You walked away and never said a word in my defense. What kind of a friend are you?"

"I'm afraid I wasn't a very good friend," Tommy said. "But I'm really sorry, and I promise you I'll never let you down again. From now on, you can count on me to be a true friend."

Danny let a smile spread across his face. "OK. I forgive you."

"You do?" Tommy was both surprised and happy.

"Of course I do," Danny said. "You are one of my best friends, and I'm not going to let one mistake end our friendship."

"Oh thank you, Danny," Tommy said. "Ever since that happened, I've been feeling like I was carrying around this big burden. I knew what Jesus would want me to do, but it was really hard to admit that I was so stupid that I didn't stand up for a good friend like you. But I knew I had to ask you to forgive me. And when you did, it was just like my burden was lifted off me. That must be what Jesus meant when he said, 'My burden is light.' Doing things Jesus's way always works out for the best."

It was summer, and there wasn't any Sunday school, so Tommy and his friends, Marvin and Danny, were waiting outside while their parents were having a cup of coffee and visiting with their friends.

"I was thinking about the sermon this morning," Tommy said. "The pastor said the story wasn't about the sower but about the soil. It seems to me that it wasn't the soil's fault that people made a path and packed the soil so the birds could come and eat it; and it wasn't the soil's fault that the gardener didn't weed out the garden so the weeds could choke the plants."

"Good point," Marvin said. "It's like some kids grow up in a home where the parents never talk about God or never have family worship times. You really can't blame the kids if the Sunday school lessons don't seem to take root."

"Yah," Danny added, "and some kids grow up in bad neighborhoods surrounded by gang-bangers and drug users and robbers. Is it really their fault that they don't know about Jesus?"

"So what is Jesus trying to tell his followers with this story?" Tommy still wasn't sure how to understand the parable.

"Look at it this way," Danny said. "Pretty soon the disciples are going to be telling about Jesus and the Kingdom of God, and not everyone they tell is going to respond the way the disciples did. So Jesus wanted them to know that there was nothing wrong with what they were saying; that's the seed they were sowing, but different people had different experiences that made them more or less likely to respond to the stories, just like the different soils responded differently to the seeds."

"And I know the pastor said Jesus wanted to make only one point with his stories," Marvin added. "But it wouldn't be a bad idea if we did a little work with the soil to make sure the seeds had a chance to grow."

The boys were choosing up sides for a baseball game at the neighborhood park. Marvin was one captain, and a kid named Harry was the other captain. Marvin knew almost all the kids, but there was one new kid. Marvin asked Tommy, "Do you think I should ask the new kid? He's pretty tall."

"He's tall all right," Tommy replied. "But he's skinny as a rail, and look at his mitt. It's right out of the dark ages. He doesn't look very athletic. I think you should pick one of the guys we know."

So Harry picked the new guy, whose name was Joe, and the game began. That afternoon, Joe played second base, caught three pop flies, made four ground outs on perfect throws to first, and one double play. He was at bat four times and hit two singles and a double, scored twice, and drove in two runs. Harry's team won 6 to 2, and there was no question that Joe was the best player on the field.

As they were walking home, Marvin had this big grin on his face and said to Tommy, "Thanks for the good advice."

Tommy laughed. "That's probably the first time I ever gave you bad advice. But seriously, it teaches us a good lesson. As the proverb goes, you can't tell a book by its cover, and you can't tell what a person can do or what they're thinking by looking at them."

"That reminds me of the story Jesus told," Marvin said. "You, remember, about the wheat and the weeds."

Tommy thought a minute. "Oh yeah, I remember. The pastor told us Jesus didn't want his followers to make judgments about people, especially about what they believed."

"Well next time," Marvin said, "you can be sure I'll try to get Joe on my team."

Tommy was asked to participate in the groundbreaking ceremony for the new church building. He would represent the young people in the congregation. Tommy felt really honored to take part in this historic event, and when it was his turn to dig a shovel of dirt, he gave a little speech that his father helped him write.

"Today, as we begin the construction of our new church building, I am participating on behalf of all the young people in our congregation. This new building will serve the needs of our generation and our children. But more important, this building will help us reach out to people in our neighborhood who have not yet heard the good news of God's love."

After the ceremony, Marvin told Tommy, "This was an exciting day, and I really liked your speech."

"Thanks, Marvin," Tommy replied. "I was just thinking about how our church has grown. Dad told me that a few years before we were born, the congregation started out in an empty storefront down at the strip mall. And then they got too big for the little store and rented the school auditorium while they built the church we're in now. Mom said I was the first baby baptized in the new church, so that means it was just ten years ago, and here we are building a new church."

"Wow," Marvin said. "Why do you think we have grown so fast?"

"It could be because we have had great pastors," Tommy replied. "But I think it's like Jesus said in our Gospel text this morning: the Kingdom of God is like a little seed that grows into a big tree. And I think that seed is *love*."

Marvin agreed. "The pastor always reminds us of God's love for us and how we should be loving toward one another. And this congregation is really good at loving. I'm glad my folks joined this church when we moved here."

Tommy smiled. "So am I."

On Saturday, Tommy, Danny, and Marvin went with their Scout troop to work at the church's food pantry. All morning long, people kept coming in looking for food to feed their families. The boys were so busy, they didn't have a moment to sit down as they filled grocery sacks with food. They were supposed to close at noon, but there were still people in line, so they kept filling orders. When the pantry closed, it was nearly 1:00 p.m.

On the way home, Marvin said, "It sure would be nice if God would make food the way Jesus did when he fed the five thousand."

"Actually," Danny said, "God has. Just yesterday I heard on the evening news that every day, we—that is, the people in America—throw away half of the food we have. I'll bet that would be enough food to feed all the hungry people in the world."

Tommy joined the conversation. "So the problem is not that there isn't enough food but that we don't get the food we have to the people who need it."

"Actually, we are working on it," Danny continued. "The news story told how many communities are organizing the supermarkets and restaurants to give the food they would throw away to homeless shelters and food pantries."

"Yah," Marvin said. "The woman in charge of the pantry said that a lot of the food we were giving away came from supermarkets."

"It's like the slogan our church had: 'God's work, our hands,'" Tommy added. "If we are followers of Jesus, we should be doing what Jesus did."

And as a result of their conversation, the boys decided to organize a food drive where the Scouts would go through the neighborhood and gather food for the food pantry.

"That was really a funny story the pastor read last Sunday." Marvin was talking about the story of Jesus walking on the water and inviting Peter to come to him.

"What was so funny about it?" Tommy asked.

"Peter!" Marvin said. "I can just see it. Peter jumps out of the boat and actually starts walking on the water, and then he looks around and sees the waves and the wind, and he thinks, 'Oh dear, what am I doing out here? I'm going to die!'" And Marvin laughed.

"I think that's the whole point of the story," Tommy said. "Jesus was going to invite his followers to do a lot of things that, to them, may have seemed impossible, and Jesus wanted them to believe that they could do it."

"Like what?" Marvin asked.

"Like forgiving people even if they hurt them seven times seventy, and not being worried about money or where their next meal was coming from, and loving their enemies and going into distant lands and telling people about Jesus."

"You're right," Marvin said. "It's like when those kids were making fun of me because I was black when I first moved here. I was really mad at them, and I found it hard to forgive them."

"But when you did," Tommy said, "you felt a lot better when you got rid of your anger, and eventually they became your friends. It just proves that even when Jesus asks us to do hard things, it turns out to be the best."

"And there is one more thing, Tommy," Marvin said. "We can do the hard stuff because Jesus promises to be with us, to help us do the right thing, just like he reached out and pulled Peter out of the water."

After school one day, Tommy saw his friend Marvin talking to a new kid who was dressed different from everyone else. Tommy called to him, and Marvin came over. "What do you want?" he asked.

"Who was that kid you were talking to?" Tommy asked.

"He's a new kid. His family just moved here from Iraq."

"How come he's dressed so funny?"

"That's the way they dress where he came from."

"What's his name?"

"Omar Rashid."

"I suppose he's a Muslim too," said Tommy. "Aren't they the people who flew planes into those buildings on 9/11?"

"They were Muslims, but not every Muslim thinks like they did. He wants to be our friend."

"I don't think I want to be his friend. He's not a Christian."

"But he is a child of God, just like you."

"I don't think so."

"Well just think about it," Marvin said. "You believe God created everything, don't you"?"

"Sure."

"Well then, if God created him, he must also be a child of God."

"Are you sure?"

"Well I'm pretty sure, why don't we ask our pastor."

Tommy's high school was getting a new football coach. He came from a school where he had won six state championships in the last ten years. In the fall, Marvin and Tommy were going to be freshmen, and both were trying out for the team. Tommy and Marvin were talking together on their way home after the first practice.

Marvin said, "Boy, isn't he a great coach? I wouldn't be surprised if we go to the state tournament this year."

"Yeah," Tommy said. "I really believe in him."

"So do I!" said Marvin.

But Marvin not only believed in him, he believed him. So when the coach said, "You boys need to get your sleep. I want you to be in bed by ten every night," Marvin went to bed at nine thirty. Tommy, on the other hand, liked to watch TV and often stayed up until 11 watching "Mash" reruns.

And when the coach said it was important to eat a good diet, Marvin made sure to eat lots of fruit and vegetables, but Tommy, not so much; he preferred candy bars and milkshakes.

And when the coach gave them a workout schedule for the weekends, Marvin ran three miles on both Saturday and Sunday. Tommy thought about it, but his favorite exercise was playing video games.

And when the coach suggested that they spend at least forty-five minutes every night studying the playbook, Marvin spent at least an hour. And Tommy? Well, he preferred to hang out with his friends; he'd study the book later. But he rarely did.

Now who do you think made the team: Tommy, who believed in the coach, or Marvin, who not only believed in the coach but believed the coach?

Tommy's mom had just told Tommy that she was free and would be happy to take Tommy and his friends to the beach. Tommy was delighted and hopped on his bike to ask Marvin and Danny if they wanted to go with him. Marvin was ready to go, but Danny was a different story.

"I promised my dad I'd help him at the community garden. We are growing fresh vegetables for the church's food pantry. I guess that's my cross to bear."

"Isn't that a little overdramatic?" Tommy asked. "I mean, when Jesus told his disciples to take up their cross and follow him, he was looking at dying on the cross. You're just giving up a day at the beach."

"Not at all," Danny replied. "When Jesus took up his cross, it was God's way of showing the world God's love and forgiveness and God's power over the forces of evil. So whatever I can do to show people God's love would be my cross. And I think helping poor people is one of the ways our church shows God's love. That's why I'm willing to give up a day at the beach."

"Now I get it," Tommy said. "When Jesus asked us to take up our cross, he wasn't asking us to die, but if we want to call ourselves his disciples, we are asked to make some sacrifices in order to show people God's love for them."

"And," Danny went on, "even us kids can do that."

One day when Tommy came home from school, he heard his sister, Lindsay, crying in her room. Tommy knocked on her door, and Lindsay said he could come in.

"Hey, sis, what's wrong?" Tommy asked.

"This morning, during the announcements," Lindsay said, "the teacher named the achievement awards, and I got the award for being the best speller. During recess, Susan blared out, so everyone could hear, that I shouldn't have won because she was the best speller in our class and I was stupid. I thought she was my friend, so it really hurt when she said that. But I knew it wouldn't do me any good to stay mad at her, so on the way home, I told her I forgave her. Instead of saying she was sorry, she started to yell at me and said she never wanted to be my friend.

"I don't know what's gotten into her. We used to be such good friends. We go to the same church, and she's even come over to our house for an overnight. I don't know what to do."

"I'll tell you what," Tommy said. "After school, you and I will go together to talk to Susan. Maybe we can find out why she's acting this way. And if that doesn't work, we'll just do what Jesus said we should do: you can bring it up in Sunday school and get the whole class involved. After that, I think you will be friends again, but if she doesn't want to, you'll just have to let her go."

"Oh I think just by having you along to talk it over will do the trick," Lindsay said. "Besides she once told me she had a crush on you, even if you are two years older."

Tommy's sister Lindsay was totally disgusted with her friend Heather. "That's the third time this week she forgot about working on our science project after school. We'll never get it done in time for the science fair. I wish I hadn't chosen her for a partner. The next day she tells me she's sorry she forgot. How many times does she expect me to forgive her?"

"Well, she probably expects you to forgive her a lot more than three times," Tommy said. "Especially since you are both in the same Sunday school class."

"What does Sunday school have to do with it?" Lindsay asked.

"Don't you remember the Gospel lesson last Sunday?" Tommy always liked it when he could remind Lindsay of something from church because she seemed to have a much better memory, or maybe she was usually paying more attention.

"Sure, I remember," Lindsay replied. "The disciples asked if it was enough to forgive seven times, and Jesus said not seven but seventy times seven. Let's see, that would be four hundred and ninety times."

"That's not the point, Lindsay. When Jesus said seven times seventy, he was using the perfect number seven. What he meant was we should always, *always*, be forgiving."

"That just doesn't sound right, Tommy."

"Look at it this way Lindsay. How many times has God forgiven you, or how many times has God forgiven me? And since God forgives us uncountable times, God expects us to be just as forgiving. It's like the king in the parable Jesus told; he forgave the servant the debt he owed him, and the king expected the servant to forgive his fellow servants."

"I guess that does make sense," Lindsay said.

One day a friend of Tommy's father, Mr. Bush, asked Tommy to mow his lawn. It was a very large lawn, and he only had a push lawnmower, so he offered to pay Tommy twenty dollars. Tommy thought that was a pretty good deal, especially since he had never made that much money in one day in his life. It was fairly cool when Tommy started mowing, but by noon it was close to 90 degrees and Tommy still had almost half the lawn to mow.

Before Tommy went home for lunch, Mr. Bush told Tommy to bring a friend to help so they could finish with the trimming that day. Tommy called his friend, Marvin, and told him he could probably make ten dollars for the afternoon, so Marvin agreed to go and help.

That afternoon, Tommy had Marvin push the lawnmower while Tommy worked with the grass clippers on the edges. It was still hard work, and when they finished by 4:30 p.m., both boys were tired and sweaty.

When they went to Mr. Bush to get paid, Mr. Bush said, "You boys worked really hard today. The lawn looks great." Then he got out his wallet and he gave Marvin a crisp new twenty dollar bill. When Tommy saw that Marvin got twenty dollars, he thought that he would get thirty or maybe even forty, but Mr. Bush gave Tommy another crisp, new twenty dollar bill.

Mr. Bush noticed that Tommy was pouting, and he said to Tommy, "Didn't you agree to mow the lawn for twenty? And so I gave you what we agreed to, besides the fact that I let you get help to finish the job. If I want to give your friend the same amount, why should you be unhappy?"

This story is like a parable that Jesus told to show people that God treats all people alike. No matter how long or how hard they worked, they had the joy of being part of God's kingdom, and God loves us all the same.

Before Tommy's father went to work one morning, he asked Tommy to weed the garden, Tommy said he was sorry, but he had a ball game and couldn't do it today. So his father asked Lindsay if she would weed the garden, and she said she would.

Lindsay was busy cleaning her room and getting her doll collection in order and decided she would weed the garden after lunch. But after lunch, it was getting really warm so she decided to wait until later in the day, but then she got busy playing at the park with her friends and forgot all about the garden.

Tommy went to the ballpark for his ball game. It turned out that the pitcher on Tommy's team was really good, or maybe the team they were playing wasn't that good, but anyway, the game was much shorter than usual and Tommy got home a little after two. When Tommy saw that the garden wasn't weeded, he decided that he would do what his father asked him to do in the morning.

Jesus told a story very much like this. At the end, he asked his disciple which one of the children did what the father asked them to do. Of course, the answer is clear. It was the one who said he would not and then he did it.

Jesus wanted to point out to his followers that it isn't enough to say you believe in God, but by the way you live you should show that you believe God by living the way Jesus taught us to live.

Jesus taught us to love all people and be nice to them and to love our parents and obey them. Can you think of other things Jesus taught us?

Tommy's next door neighbor, Mrs. Adams, asked him if he would like to earn twenty-five dollars during the summer. Of course, Tommy said yes. "What do I have to do?" he asked.

"I have this beautiful orchid plant, and it will be in full bloom while we are in Germany for a month," Mrs. Adams said. "All you have to do is give it a little water once a week and mist it with a little spray bottle I'll give you."

"I'm sure I can do that, Mrs. Adams," Tommy said. And so the next day, Mrs. Adams brought the plant over to Tommy's house with a little slip of paper with the instructions on how to take care of the orchid. "You won't forget about my little plant," she said, and Tommy assured her that he wouldn't.

Summer is a busy time for young boys. There are baseball games and weekend camping trips. Even so, Tommy did remember the first week. But the second week he went on a camping trip with his Boy Scout troop, and after that, he completely forgot all about the orchid.

The next month, the doorbell rang, and when Tommy looked out the window and saw Mrs. Adams, he remembered the orchid. He ran to the guest bedroom where he had put it next to the window, but it didn't look very good at all. The blossoms had all dried up, and the leaves were wilted.

When he took the plant to Mrs. Adams, she was very upset. "What do you think I should do?" she asked Tommy.

"I guess you shouldn't pay me." Tommy said. And that's exactly what Mrs. Adams did.

Jesus told a story like this to show the chief priests and Pharisees that they hadn't taken very good care of God's church. How can we take care of God's church?

"Hey, Tommy." Marvin came running across the playground. "I was just talking to Henry, and he said you and I are going to the wrong church and therefore we're going to go to hell. What do you think about that?"

"All I can say is I hope his pastor didn't teach him that. Our pastor says there are a lot of different ideas about how to worship and how to understand different parts of the Bible, but that there is room for all these different people in the Kingdom of God."

"I sure hope our pastor is right," Marvin said. "It didn't feel very good to have someone say I was going to hell."

"I wouldn't worry about that, Marvin. What's more important is making sure you are learning how to be a follower of Jesus right now."

"What do you mean?" Marvin asked

"Well, the way I understand it," Tommy said, "is that Jesus came to teach us how God wants us to live. Not just to follow a bunch of rules so we can get to heaven, but to discover what life is all about and to become the people we were created to be and to discover how beautiful and satisfying life can be. Jesus called it being a follower of the way."

"That just sounds like a lot of fancy talk," Marvin said. "Give me an example of what you're talking about."

"OK," Tommy said. "The Bible tells us that we are all created by God. You are a child of God, I am a child of God, and every human being is a child of God. That means every person on earth is my brother and sister. So to begin with, I will try to love and care for others. That's being a follower of the way."

It was the Fourth of July and Danny, Marvin, and Tommy were downtown watching the parade. It was the biggest parade of the year, with marching bands from a dozen high schools, and fire trucks and horses and floats from all the different organizations in town. The senior class and the junior class both had floats, as well as the American Legion and the Veterans of Foreign Wars and a lot of the churches.

Just then, the float from the church the boys belonged to went by, and the boys cheered and waved to their friends. The float had a thanksgiving theme, portraying the many things we have to be thankful for in America.

"I'm sure glad I live in the United States," Tommy said, "and not some country where they make everyone worship the same way."

"Are there really places like that?" Marvin asked.

"There are," Danny said. "And even worse, my father was telling me about a minister's son in East Germany when it was under the control of Russia. He had to make a really hard choice. If he wanted to continue his education as a piano player, he had to say he didn't believe in God."

"What would you do if you had to make that kind of choice?" Marvin asked Tommy.

"I'm just glad I don't have to," Tommy replied. "In the United States, our Constitution says that everybody can worship the way they want to and no one can ever stop us from worshiping God."

"We sure have a lot to be thankful for living where we do," Marvin said.

And both Tommy and Danny said, "Amen!"

One day, Tommy saw his friend Danny mowing Witchy Wilson's lawn. They called Mrs. Wilson "Witchy Wilson" because she was so mean. "Hey, Danny," Tommy said, "what are you doing mowing Witchy Wilson's lawn? She must be paying you a fortune to get you to work for her."

"She isn't paying me anything," Danny replied. "I'm doing it as a favor to her."

"So you're being good for nothing." Tommy laughed.

"And just because the other kids call her Witchy Wilson," Danny said, "you shouldn't. It's not very kind."

"Well didn't she call the cops on you just because you rode your bike through her yard?"

"Yeah, she did, but she had a right to. I almost rode over one of her flower beds."

"So how come you're mowing her lawn?" Tommy asked.

"Remember the Sunday school lesson we had when the teacher read out of the Bible that we should love our enemies and do good to those who hate us?" Danny asked.

"Yeah," Tommy said, "but I think that's dumb."

"I thought so too, but then I thought I'd try it out," Danny said. "So one hot day when I saw Mrs. Wilson pushing that old lawn mower of hers, I offered to finish mowing the lawn for her. She was really glad to let me finish, and when I got done, she invited me up on the porch for milk and homemade chocolate cookies. And while we ate the cookies, we talked, and I found out she's not really a mean person; she's just lonely. She doesn't have any grandchildren, and her husband died a few years ago. So I decided to adopt her as my grandmother, and I've been mowing her lawn ever since. She even lets me cut through her yard now, as long as I'm careful not to run over her flowers. Look, there she is on the porch now. I bet she'll let you have some cookies too."

Pastor Gil

Tommy and Marvin were walking home from Little League baseball practice. "I really feel good about the practice this afternoon," Marvin said. "The coach gave me some good tips about the way I stand when I'm hitting, and I think I got about twice as many hits during batting practice."

"You sure did," Tommy said. "I was in the outfield when you were up to bat, and you had me chasing balls all over the place. You were almost as good a hitter as Larry."

"Thanks for the compliment, pal," Marvin said. "Larry is by far the best player on the team, but why does the coach get on his case all the time? I bet coach is correcting him more than any other kid on the team."

"Yeah," Tommy said. "He's certainly the tallest and strongest kid on the team. Playing baseball comes easy for him, but sometimes that's a problem. He doesn't have to work hard, and so he doesn't, and then he doesn't pay attention to what he's doing or he starts showing off. And then he makes an error."

"I think you're right, Tommy. The coach knows that he could be the best player in the whole city if he wasn't so full of himself. He was born to play baseball, and now the coach wants him to develop his skills and become the best."

"You know," Tommy said, "it kind of reminds me of the Pharisees and Jesus. The Pharisees knew the Bible better than anyone. They knew all the commandments, and they spent a lot of time in church praying and stuff. But Jesus was always getting after them. I think it was because they were so close to being on the right path, but they missed the main point. Instead of thinking about others and how they could be helpful, they thought only of themselves and how good they were. So just like the coach gets after Larry, Jesus went after the Pharisees."

Tommy and Marvin were discussing the Boy Scout motto "Be Prepared." Tommy asked, "What does it mean to be prepared, and what are we supposed to be prepared for?"

Marvin thought for a moment. "I remember our scoutmaster said that to be prepared meant we should develop our minds, bodies, and spirits so we are ready for any kind of challenge we might face."

Tommy also began to remember. "So that's why we have programs in scouting that make our bodies stronger, like lifesaving and hiking and climbing."

"Yes," Marvin said, "and why we have programs like reading and chemistry and electronics to develop our minds."

"But what about developing our spirits?" Tommy asked. "I can't think of any programs for developing our spirits."

"How do we develop our spirits?" Marvin wondered. "Like the story Jesus told about the maidens who ran out of oil for their lamps. It's pretty clear Jesus wasn't talking about having enough oil. How do we prepare our spirits?"

Both boys thought for a few moments, and then Tommy came up with an idea. "To begin with, I would think we need to get familiar with the lessons Jesus taught his disciples. What would you think are his most important lessons?"

"Well, one time Jesus said the first thing is to love God," Marvin began. "And the second thing is to love our neighbors as ourselves, so I would say that we begin being spiritually prepared by recognizing that we are connected to God and our neighbors, like members of a great family. And because we're connected, we should care about them."

"Wow!" Tommy was impressed. "You sure come up with some amazing ideas."

One day in early summer, Tommy's friend, Marvin, saw Tommy working in a garden about two blocks away from Tommy's house. "Hey, Tommy, what are you doing in that garden?" Marvin asked.

"I'm hoeing," Tommy said.

"Why?" Marvin asked. "Is it your garden?"

"Well not exactly," Tommy said. "I mean the land belongs to Mr. Johnson, but he lets us use it without charging us anything. He just likes to see the land being put to good use."

"Oh, you're stewards of the garden," Marvin said.

"We're what?" Tommy asked.

"Stewards. Don't you remember in Sunday school when the teacher was explaining to us about stewards in the Bible? A steward is someone who takes care of someone else's property like it is his own. Our teacher said we are stewards of creation. We are God's caretakers."

"Now I understand what she was talking about. It's like Mr. Johnson owns the land, but he lets us plant a garden there, and we can plant anything we want. And when we harvest the food, it's ours to use, although he does like it when we drop off a bag of tomatoes and cucumbers. In the same way, God has put us in charge of the earth. It's ours to use, to make decisions about how to use it, but it still belongs to God."

"That's right," Marvin said, "and that's why I called you a steward of the garden."

Pastor Gil

Tommy and Danny were going into church one Sunday morning when they saw a boy about their age sitting on a bench by the front door. He didn't look like he was going to Sunday school. His clothes were smudged with dirt, and his hair was all messed up.

"Do you know that kid?" Tommy asked.

"No," Danny replied. "He probably belongs to a family that spent the night at church."

"Spent the night at church?" Tommy was puzzled. "Why would his family spend the night at church?"

"Don't you remember? Our church provides a shelter for homeless people."

Tommy thought it was strange for people to spend the night at church. They didn't even have a shower, although they did have a nice kitchen to fix breakfast. Danny explained that providing shelter was part of the church's ministry to care for the poor and the sick and the homeless. "After all, Jesus said when we visit the sick and feed the hungry and clothe the naked, it's as if we were doing it for Jesus. I guess you didn't recognize Jesus sitting outside."

Tommy smiled. "No, I didn't. I think it's great that we provide shelter for the homeless. In fact, I'm going back outside to invite 'Jesus' to join us for Sunday school, if it's all right with his parents. We have a lot more to give than food and shelter."

I hope you have enjoyed reading about Tommy and his friends. Remember to look for *What Was Tommy Thinking? Cycle B* at your favorite religious bookstore to discover more about the Gospel readings for each Sunday.

ABOUT THE AUTHOR

Pastor Gil has been drawing pictures as far back as he can remember. He attended grade school in a country school that didn't have an art teacher but they got lessons in drawing from a public radio program called "Let's Draw." The pictures they drew were sent to the University of Wisconsin Art Department and with their responses of encouragement Gil was on his way. In his middle school and high school years Gil lived in a larger city that had art teachers and even though there wasn't room for an art class in the college prep track, he gave up his study halls to include them.

In high school he did the art work in the school annual, at the University of Wisconsin he designed the homecoming button and in seminary he again did the artwork for the yearbook. He also did the artwork for a youth ministry manual where he created his Tommy character. As a seminary student, Gil visited Bethel Lutheran Church in Madison which was in the process of developing the Bethel Bible Study program. Gil was impressed with the effectiveness of using pictures to reinforce learning.

Pastor Gil's first parish was in a small mining town north of Spokane, WA. It was here that he began telling stories about a young boy named Tommy who found insights for his own life in the Gospel lessons on Sunday morning.

For the next fifteen years Pastor Gil served as a campus pastor at Central Washington State, University of Southern California and University of Montana. As a University student himself and as a Campus pastor, he responded to the new knowledge constantly being discovered, not as a challenge to faith but as a window to new and even more profound insights into God and creation. In writing his stories Pastor Gil's goal is to set forth a theological background that will stand up when the child moves from Sunday School to the University.

Printed in the United States
By Bookmasters